Poems In Which I Am Chopped Up, Stepped On, and Sleep Deprived

Zack Rearick

Purchase more copies of this book online:

Etched Press
www.etchedpress.com

Also available in Amazon Kindle Store

ACKNOWLEDGMENTS

To everyone who contributed to the creation or refining of this book (in whatever way): Jamie, Sarah, Steve, and Snowy. To Kevin, who thinks more highly of my poetry than I do. To my poet-sisters, Anne and Elizabeth. To Kelly, my always-editor, who didn't actually edit this book, but may as well have. To Christen, the love of my life and the woman who has forever silenced the voice in which these poems were written. And to my parents, without whom I could do nothing.

TABLE OF CONTENTS

Doctor: What is it you strive for?

A. S.: Someone to look at me and tell me I'm all right — or to hit me.

–Taped therapy conversation between Anne Sexton and Dr. Martin Orne, January 16, 1962

Shoebottom Solstice

This is not the summer of self-hatred
(though if it was you'd be the first to know).
The late June sun, when it is at its apex,
predicts its nonexistent afterglow.

I've heard it said that being stomped to death
is the most brutal way a man can die,
the flattened lung's last begging, coughing breath,
the pulpy face, the heel against the eye.

The gruesomeness is attributable
not simply to violence of the scene
(for other deaths have fractured ribs and skulls,
and every murder is, of course, obscene),

but to the repetition it demands
to bring one's foot down on a human frame,
to gaze upon a halfway mashed-in man
and to persist with equal force and aim.

I've been the man in question more than once,
have laid down often by my own design,
waiting for a pair of boots or pumps
to notice me and feel this way inclined.

I'll trick you into filling that position
if you don't keep an eye on where you step.
I'll use you to further my condition
and my own aesthetic of helplessness.

You mean so well that you miss the unspoken,

irradiant will to die with which I beam.
I am so lonely that it lays me open.
Your friendly toes reduce my heart to cream.

So as I foam and spill on your shoelaces,
ignore my feigned, misleading cries for help.
This is not a moment of self-hatred,
it is the searing twilight of the self.

Instead, the Stick

I have a big, black spider on my brain.
He spreads himself like a crack or a raincloud.
He drizzles venom.

At first, I thought to ask for help.
I told my friends and parents how he'd talk to me.
When a spider speaks, it is in an evil baritone with a tittering,
high-pitched echo.
It sounds how you imagine a tornado would if it were
speaking.
I journaled his words and observations like they asked me to.
He would tell me things that were wrong with me.
He would never stop.

They sent me to a therapist.
She told me I had made the spider up.
She told me I had many positive qualities.
She told me not to think badly of myself.
The spider snickered and danced around.
He said that, if anything, he had made *me* up.
He knew a lot of words I didn't know.

My therapist was fooled by my perceptivity.
She thought it meant I was learning the truth about myself.
I only did what the spider told me to do.
He was very clever.
My therapist declared me fully healed.
The spider was proud and puffed up like a cat.

I still thought maybe I could get away from him.
I had to plan in secret.

I knew my only chance was to see a doctor.
I had a routine check-up planned already,
so the spider was not suspicious.
When we got there, I screamed
that I had something in my head that had to be removed.
The doctor was afraid of me.
He opened up my skull with a shiny knife.
The spider never panicked.
He scuttled to the underside of my brain.
The doctor couldn't see him, even with his flashlight.

When I got home, the spider said I needed to be punished.
He made himself twice as large.
The reverb from his voice gave me a headache.
He told me that I had to hurt myself.
He told me no one cared about me anyway.

I have a big, black spider on my brain.
He's been there longer than I can remember.
He coughs loudly when people try to say nice things about me.
He uses his fangs when I try to help myself.
He catalogues my failures.
I don't suppose there's anything to do.
I don't suppose you'll ever see him either.

Or a Mouse

Do anything to me,
do anything to me,
do anything to me,
but do it gently.

Do anything to me,
do anything to me,
do anything to me.
I live too simply.

So let the endless rug
be level with my head,
and let the insides of
the walls surround me.

You ran me like a bug
into my coffin-bed,
and your heel stirred up the
dust which floats around me.

A sentimental shrug
at the fact that I am dead
is all that I'll deserve
when they have found me.

Three Letters

I. Letter Written While Biking Home From Campus

(Enclosed is the following quote from Maxine Kumin,
speaking about her friend Anne Sexton: "Anne always had
the notion that she was the most underloved person in the
universe...There could never be enough proof that she was
loved.")

How are you this early evening?
How's the week been going?
Today's like any other day in early April,
only colder.
I haven't heard from you in a while.
I've had to wear a jacket.
You've fathered me like James Wright,
saying you'll get your list of my positive traits to me later.
Mothered me.
The flowers I pass are a malicious pink.
They spin on their stalks like nightmares.
They have an alluring momentum.

Well, spring has come as they said it would.
It was only a few weeks late.
I will not be attending.
God has had little to do with it.
I crossed a busy street. The world seemed less solid.
I pushed my pedals, but didn't move.
Traffic failed to stop for me.

My hands are hard to feel as I compose this.
A ghost is a thing that's dead and has returned.

I didn't need so many flowers,
I needed to hear something other than *later*.
All dogs bark at me. I'm finished.

Oh God, I'm Anne Sexton.

II. Letter Written While Imitating Maria DiBenigno

(Enclosed is the following quote from Elizabeth, Anne Sexton's temporary second personality, speaking about Sexton herself to her therapist Dr. Martin Orne: "She acts her life away.")

What are things like for you?
What have you heard?
There are many things to say about me.
I have no sense of privacy. I have nothing to hide.

When are we happiest,
at the end of a breath or the beginning?
My breathing gets shallower as yours gets shallower.
My eyes widen as yours widen.
Expect this of me. I'm a mimicker. I mimic.

How does one survive?
I pace my living room
and break my hand against my other hand.
How do you survive as you?
I'm sure there is a secret.
I never turn the lights on at my place.
There isn't anything to see.
I don't even have a dog.
Because I would become like a dog.

I am in that sense subhuman. Non-human.

Build me however you like.
When you're done, you can blow me away like eraser-dust.
You can start from scratch. You can ghostwrite me.
You can make me say anything.
My voice has no distinctives.
I don't speak with the timbre of my times.
Listen to me. Listen to me!

Whatever you do, don't believe a word of it.

III. *Letter Written While Watching* Hellraiser 2

(Enclosed is the following quote from Anne Sexton, speaking to Dr. Orne: "I am nothing if not an actress off stage. In fact, it comes down to the terrible truth that there is no true part of me.")

Have you been sleeping well?
I haven't.
Have you been dreaming dreams of blood?
Don't be scared of me. Some of us are born skinless.
It doesn't mean we aren't people.

Does it? How thick is a nightmare?
How many are too many?
The word *fretted* was invented for insomniacs.
When I say I'm having trouble sleeping,
I mean that I'm afraid to see what I will be
when I wake in the morning. Who I will be.

When you ask me if I've been missing sleep,
it sounds so innocent. I have been.
My heart has been pounding harder as each day darkens.
Night has been dragging itself across my face.
I have been waking involuntarily at the same time every
morning.
It's important for me that you know it's involuntary.

Thank you for your concern.
You wouldn't mind if I shaved you of yourself?
If I dressed in you?
If I unplugged my alarm after?

Please help me. I'm in hell.

IV. Postscript to the Third Letter (Lionfish Drive)

I took apart my flesh one day
to better know myself
and dug below my bones and charms,
my sympathies and spells,

but found no thing but nothingness
recoiling underneath.
How have I since corrected this
and gathered unto me

that thing which true sincerity
cannot exist without?
I've skinned you of your personhood
and worn the garment out.

Partnering

Take me out.
Let's go to the big ballroom againagain,
and we'll see in the ceiling, in the rotunda,
slivers of blue like skyspit,
cobalt. Go waltz.
Take me to the mirrored floor
and show me off. I want everyone to see
me and you paralleled
with our upsidedown compatriots
who never stop fighting.
Take me out. Let's go there
and tango ourselves orange.
We'll look up and down with roses in our mouths,
and there will be thorns between our teeth.
You'll dip me fuller than Achilles.
I don't know how to rhumba
or anything else.
Take me through those silver doors
where everyone waits to see us.
We'll jitterbug like lunatics.
We'll twist 'til we're too tight together.
We'll do the Harlem Shake while it's still in style.
The clapping will keep us going.
Until we stop dancing. Is it still in style?
Are the lights too hot for you too?
Did you see their heads shake? Is it still in style?
Take me out so we can make them happy. Take me,

take me to the door.
I don't wanna dance no more.

The Hacking

One day, you just got fed up with the whole thing.
You stormed out of our bedroom
and down the stairs to the back door.
Walking to the shed, the soft white   crunchcrunchhhhhh
crushed.
You ripped the ax off the wall.
It had been snowing for three weeks,
despite forecasts to the contrary.
I watched you from the frostruined window
disappearing blurrily back into the kitchen.

We met on the middle step.
I didn't get past the *What's*—
before you hit me square in the mouth with it.
I tumbled down the stairs like a bag of laundry.
The bruises on my arms were the color of squashed grapes.

I sat up and attempted to speak,
but my lips tore in four
and flapped uselessly by my chin.
You struck me in the side of skull, by my left ear.

Whack!
My forehead split and my brain gurgled
Whack!
My right eye popped and my left one was caught on the corner
Whack!
My head hung to the side
and my dead tongue moved to lie
and the red stung useless eyes
Whack!

You started on my torso

I crawled away so I could crawl back to you.
I raised my hand in one weak, begging motion,
creating a little wall of pity between you and me and
it and

Whack!
You only missed my thumb and index finger
Whack!
which doesn't matter if my whole hand's gone
Whack!
which doesn't matter if my whole arm's gone
Whack!
Another shot to the chest

I began dragging myself to the kitchen to make you some tea.
I knew you liked to have a cup or two when you were stressed.
I got all the way to the fridge before

Whack!
My left leg was phantomed below the kneecap
Whack!
My right arm spun off and sputtered
Whack!
My blood slunk apologetically across the linoleum
Whack!
My ribcage splintered like balsa wood

I wagged my tongue frantically to let you know
I understood and empathized.
You were without mercy.
Using my one hand, I grabbed a handful of paper towels
to wipe the mess off your slippers.
You sighed and

Whack!

My severed hand curled up by the toastet
Whack!
My severed head thrown up on the table
Whack!
Bits of my toes in the kitty dish
Whack!
Another shot to the chest

I used my remaining appendage to

Whack!
You
Whack!
hit
Whack!
me
Whack!
hard
Whack!
and
Whack!
harder
Whack!
until

finally nothing was left but my heart,
trembling with fear and with anger,
which you picked up, cleaned off,
and took back upstairs with you, contented.

In its final act, my mangled head made sure
the napkins were arranged properly.

Buddies

after Furry Lewis

Death is not a fast, grey wolf.
He is a mewing kitten
who whines when not attended to
and howls when he is bitten.

Death is unsure of himself.
He longs to be invited
into your house, but never is.
He constantly feels slighted.

Death has many therapists.
He tries to be himself.
I think I like him most because
he seems to need my help.

The Heavy Heart, Heavy Head,
Ingrid Bergman Blues

after Lightnin' Hopkins

I've been killing myself
in poems
for over a year now.
I think about it
during class.
At the end of the day,
I bike back to myself
and spread four or five poems
on the floor in front of me
and set them off
simultaneously.

I don't keep them
in my bedroom
for this very reason.
Once they've been started,
they jump at my neck like rottweilers.
I get on my knees to let them at me.
They chew on my jugular for hours.

Later, I watch the whole affair again
with a bowl of popcorn and a drink.
I like that it's in black and white.
I like that the great actresses
of the 40s and 50s
come in at the end to dress
my wounds. I like that
the scraps of me are wadded
and stuffed in a corner.

I like that no one is quick enough
to save me.
you you you you
as joan of arc
lending me your sword
lopping off your hair
leading me to fire

cher ami, bon soldat
dear friend good soldier

The Empty Couch, Two Years Since I Kissed a Girl Blossom Dearie Blues

after Howlin' Wolf

What woman wants a man
like me?
No woman that I know.
I have my charms, though.
They've told me.
I can see the insides

of girls from the outside.
I prefer kissing to sex.
No one's ever asked me
to stop yelling.
No one's ever lost me.

I've lost
a few.
Mostly just ex-girlfriends.
The last girl who turned me down
asked me not to write
a poem about it.
I didn't.
She said I wasn't her type, which I know
is the kindest possible way

for a girl to tell a guy he's unattractive.
But I don't need to be attractive.
It isn't important to me.
I need to be necessary.
Most of the girls
I've dated or gone on dates with

won't speak to me now.
It always feels like I'm losing
a new sister,
which is probably why they leave
in the first place.

you you you you
as lost lover
asking me to wait
turning off your phone
softening my sorrow

touch the hand of love
as you travel your
tomorrows alone

Nightmare Girl

Once she wanted me to exorcise
her self-possession,
and then failing that she wanted lies
and vivisection.

                                     -Aimee Mann, "Nightmare Girl"

   A thinking woman sleeps with monsters.
                   -Adrienne Rich, "Snapshots of a Daughter-In-Law"

You came in through the window,
of course. You flew.
Nothing to tell me, no sound was made.
Outside, the rain came all at once
like someone broke a glass sky. It was cinematic.
There was a laugh track
that hadn't been updated in decades.
I could hear my dead grandfather in it.

I was in my bed, uncharacteristically.
No one was with me.
The wall yawned, the wall yawned.
It was night; I forget to tell people.
The room had a little light,
call it a remnant. Your hand
made several shadows. Your hand
came up from the end of the bed and was over me. Your hand
was bigger than my whole body. Your hand
was a claw.

And I sat up, wanting to
see you better, wanting to

brush the thin strands
of shadow from your face.
You had witch's hair and Cossack teeth.
Your nails were thick, your wings were wide.
Your skin was an ugly green.
You were only a nightmare.

And I sit up, thinking excessively,
unaware for a moment that you'd
clutched onto the fever of my fear
and pulled yourself out.
Your first sickly breath was a reification,
your second landed on my neck.

And now I sit up, thinking to run,
and the stars, late as always,
scream a million tinny silver warnings.

You are too quick for me.
I can find no escape
and hope only to beat you back with my pillows.
You eat them like sleeping pills,
but you and I will be insomniacs forever,
awake forever, no matter what the doctors say.
You and I will be one and you whistle
at the thought and you know me now.
You know where I keep my trash,
where I keep my keys,
where I keep my nail polish,

you know about
this fantasy I have about
a casket door shutting on me,

the tears and well-wishes and regrets of the ones I love
soaking into the earth and making it sweet,
the nails coming down around me
like a hail storm, never touching me,
the fulfillment that comes
with being permanently surrounded,
(Most people are afraid to be buried alive, but I'm not.
I worry that all this air might smother me.)

you know about
this fantasy I have about
being stamped on by a girl
wearing high heels,
feeling each new puncture
pleasurably,
being ground into the floor,
being below you,
being beneath you,
being so full of holes
that no one could expect me
to retain anything.

You undo me like
a braid, it's so easy.
Everything that's wrong with me:
I am not a good person.
I eat poorly. I am no good at praying.
I worry ceaselessly. I am a sucker for shame.
I am too lazy to keep my apartment clean.
I can't eat breakfast without getting sick.
I lie to keep conversations moving.
I hate being single because I hate myself.
I never say anything meaningful to God.

I refuse to speak up when I'm being stepped on.
I leave the worst voicemails
I can't stay angry for more than three minutes.
I can't ask for help for fear of bothering people.
I can't trust that I won't be abandoned.
I can't let go of bad relationships.
I nod whether or not I actually understand.
I never improve. I never learn. I used to bite my fingers
when I'd get stressed to calm myself down
and I still do. I don't do push-ups. I don't act responsibly.
I am wasteful. I am melodramatic.
I am obsessive. I am weaker than any other man.
I am dangerously incautious in love
even though I know better.
I am not a good person.
I cry in the shower. I cry during lunch.
I cry in the car. I cry between breaths. I cry weekly.
I cry at old movies. I cry at new movies.
I cry over anything. I'm too forgiving.
I'm too obliging. I'm too emotional.
I am not worth it. I am boundry-less. I can't stop
speaking when I'm nervous. I can't stop
speaking when I'm happy. I can't stop
speaking when there's quiet.
I have a voice in my head that taunts me mercilessly.
I have panic attacks if I'm alone for more than 8 hours.
I have panic attacks if I'm criticized by someone who matters.
I have to fantasize about people saying nice things about me
every night because it's the only way I can get to sleep.
I have to find someone to fall in love with me in the next 5 years
or I will kill myself, and I can't be talked out of it.
I am deeply ugly.
I am fat with contradictions.

I hate all men before I get to know them.
I will do anything a pretty girl asks me to.
I may have repressed most of my adolescence.
I may have given up on my little sister too easily.
I may have pretended to need therapy for the attention.
I may need therapy now.
I may have fabricated earlier portions of this poem.
I am fear and want and failure
and failure to want.
I am not a good person.
My parents don't know
that I want to be a girl.
My father doesn't know
that I can't forgive him for being an adulterer.
My mother doesn't know
that I'm making all of her mistakes.
My little brother doesn't know
not to look up to me.
My best friend doesn't know
when he hurts me because I never tell him.
My last therapist doesn't know
that I only listened to her because she was a beautiful woman.
My ex-girlfriends don't know
for sure that I was sexually attracted to them.
No one in Wilmington knows
that when I come home
I lock the door quickly and
press my back against it and
hold my hands to my chest like something's chasing me.
No one knows who I am
because there is nothing
to know.
No one who loves me knows

anything about me,
which is how it must be.

You don't reply because
your upper and lower jaw
are now several feet apart.
You tilt the room,
and I slide into your mouth
and I wake up in the bathtub,
the water long past tepid,
and it has a top like a coffin
and I'm not strong enough to move it
and I'm drowning and my electric razor's buzzing

and I wake up in the ocean,
lost forever,
abandoned by my shipmates
and the girl who said we'd
go diving for something valuable,
and that looks like a stormcloud
and that looks like a bolt of lightning
and that looks like the sharks
they show in movies

and I wake up in a swamp in Louisiana
next to the eyes of an alligator
who has somehow learned
that the stock footage of one of his ancestors
from the opening of 1954's *Creature from the Black Lagoon*
made me squirm in my living room,
and he chuckles and he has a human voice
and he speaks with a British accent and he says
Good evening, sir.

I'm going to chew you into nothing
like a frog or a small bird,
and then the thrashing starts

and I wake up in my bed
(it was sweat all along)
and see that I've been
asleep
for less
than an hour.
I have to go back,
I have a test tomorrow
in the morning

or is it Tuesday?
What month is this?
I think there's a class
I've been forgetting to attend all semester,
I think the test was given yesterday,
I think I have to give a speech in fifteen minutes,

I think there's someone under the covers with me,
I think my legs are being swallowed,
I think that's how being bitten feels,

what if I loved you?
What if I loved you?
What if I loNo

nonononononononoyourteeth
turn me over.

Nonononononononotheheat
of your mouth is awful.

Nonononononononopleasedont
let it get me, please!

NonononononononoandI
wake up inside you.

www.ingramcontent.com/pod-product-compliance
Lightning Source LLC
Chambersburg PA
CBHW051742040426
42447CB00008B/1261